C000152709

STAMPS

THE COLLECTOR'S CORNER

STAMPS

Grange
BOOKS

A Quantum Book

Published by Grange Books
an imprint of Grange Books Plc
The Grange
Kingsnorth Industrial Estate
Hoo, nr Rochester
Kent ME3 9ND

ISBN 1-84013-299-X

This book is produced by
Quantum Books Ltd
6 Blundell Street
London N7 9BH

Project Manager: Rebecca Kingsley
Art Director: Siân Keogh
Project Editor: Jo Wells
Designer: Martin Laurie
Editor: Lyn Coutts

The material in this publication previously appeared in
The Beginner's Guide to Stamp Collecting

QUMCCSP
Set in Gill Sans
Reproduced in Singapore by Eray Scan Pte Ltd
Printed in Singapore by Star Standard Industries (Pte) Ltd

CONTENTS

THE EARLY DAYS

• • • •

The postal services established in the seventeenth century in Great Britain laid the foundations for similar post offices around the world. Originally, the only letters carried were those to and from the King and the royal court. The first public post was started in 1626, between London and Plymouth. Soon other services began and a network grew between the main cities. On 31 July, 1635 King Charles I issued a proclamation extending the use of the Royal Mail to the public. At first all letters had to be carried to London, Edinburgh or Dublin to be forwarded on, but additional 'cross' routes were eventually established.

The first postmarks

In 1660 Henry Bishop was made Postmaster General and he introduced the first postmark in 1661. The Bishop mark, as it is called, showed the day and the

BELOW A Bishop mark on the back of a letter sent to Norfolk, England, in 1693.

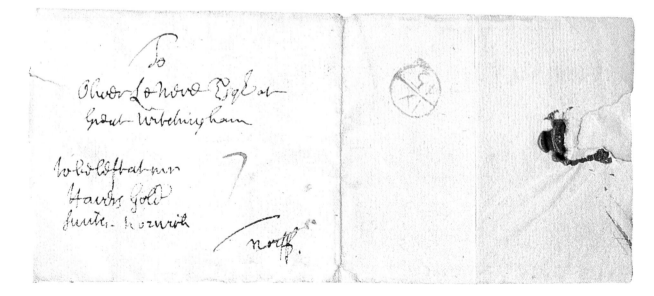

month of posting, and its purpose was to ensure that the letter carriers did not delay the mail. Similar postmarks were also used in America where they are called American Bishop marks or Franklin marks.

Postal rates and routes

Early postal rates were very complicated. The cost of sending a letter was calculated on the distance travelled and on the number of sheets of paper included in the letter. The whole process was very time-consuming and expensive. Only the rich and businesses could afford to use the post. Over the years the costs reduced and the post became a service for all.

The penny post

A special local penny post was introduced in London in 1680 by William Dockwra. His service also introduced the first prepayment of letters – previously the practice had been for the recipient to pay for the cost of the letter. This cheap local post was soon used in other major cities and was later adopted by many towns.

Revenue from the post went to the Government. The London penny post was increased to twopence in 1801 to help finance the war against Napoleon.

Rowland Hill's reforms

The man who pioneered the greatest postal reforms was Rowland Hill. His dream, which he was finally able to fulfil, was to have a cheap and efficient postal system which everybody could afford to use. He was also keen to introduce a convenient method of prepaying the postage and suggested 'a bit of paper just large enough to bear a stamp, and covered at the back with a glutinous wash'.

Rowland Hill demonstrated that the cost of transporting a letter from one post town to another was almost negligible. He also showed that it would be far better to charge for the service by weight rather than by the number of sheets. He suggested that there should be a uniform charge of one penny per half ounce made on all letters delivered within the United Kingdom and that payment could be prepaid by using a label or special stationery.

His recommendations were approved and in 1839 a competition to design adhesive labels and stamped paper was organized. The best of the 2,600 entries (none of which were totally suitable) were refined by Rowland Hill himself, with the help of the printers Perkins, Bacon and Petch.

However, the public demand for a uniform penny post was so great that the new postal rates were introduced on 10 January, 1840, several months ahead of schedule and well before any postage stamps were ready. Special handstamps had to be made for use by the post offices to indicate that the penny postage had been paid.

Finally on 6 May, 1840 stamped wrappers designed by William Mulready and the famous Penny Black stamps were on sale at post offices. The twopenny stamp was not ready until 8 May.

It was initially thought that Mulready's pre-stamped wrappers would be used more frequently than the adhesive stamps. But the design was ridiculed by all and the penny and twopenny stamps were by far the most popular.

Overseas post offices

After the issue of the first stamps, many of the British colonies expressed a wish to issue their own postage stamps. However, the General Post Office (GPO) in London at first dismissed this idea, because it was thought that it would be too confusing if more than one country were to use them. The GPO believed that the postal workers would not be able to cope if hundreds of different postage stamps were available. So the first stamps which these colonies were allowed was a standard handstamp applied in red on letters. It showed a crown on top of a circle with the words 'PAID AT' and the name of the city or country.

RIGHT Early postal stationery with a stamp printed or embossed to show that the postage has been prepaid.

Other countries were not so restricted, and it was not very long before adhesive stamps were appearing on post elsewhere around the world. Brazil followed Great Britain on 1 August, 1843 with the issue of the famous 'Bull's Eye' stamps. The cantons (states) of Switzerland came next with their first stamp issues in 1843 and 1845. These were followed by the United States of America and Mauritius in 1847 and France, Belgium and Bavaria in 1849.

Unusual methods of transporting the mail

Sending a letter has not always meant popping it into a slot or box. Even within the last 50 years unusual methods of sending, moving and delivering mail have been used, particularly in the more remote corners of the world. Many local variations have been used since the tradition of sending mail began and strange means of transport were employed to link more remote areas with the proper postal routes. For example, in the Australian bush a cyclist had to pedal over a hundred miles with the mail. 'Rocket mail' attempted to span rivers by attaching the letters and parcels to a rocket.

St Helena is a remote island in the middle of the South Atlantic Ocean. Its position made it a good place for ships travelling long distances to stop and replenish their supplies of water. At the same time, the sailors would drop off letters that had to be forwarded to other countries. Before the post office was opened in 1815, these letters would be left for collection under special

stones. The next ship to call would take any letters addressed to its country of destination onwards on their journey.

In Tonga, a group of Pacific islands, small boats carried the mail out to ships sealed in a tin can. Before this swimmers had made the risky journey from the islands out to the vessels. This was known as the 'Tin Can Mail'.

The 'Balloon Post' sent letters soaring into the air in balloons in order to get mail out of Paris when the city was under siege during the Franco-Prussian war between 1870 and 1871. Of the 56 balloons that were floated out of the capital, 51 eventually carried their cargo to the outside world.

During the same siege, other attempts to get mail out of Paris included sending it down the river in sealed canisters or metal balls. Many canisters were lost by this desperate method.

LEFT AND ABOVE
The first stamps the penny black and twopenny blue (above) were re-designed and replaced in 1841 by the brand new penny red and improved twopenny blue (left).

UNIVERSAL POSTAL UNION

On 9 October, 1874, at the end of a conference which was held in Berne, Switzerland, the General Postal Union was founded, with 22 countries as members. Austria, Hungary, Belgium, Egypt, Denmark, France, Italy, Greece, Germany, Great Britain, Luxembourg, Portugal, the Netherlands, Norway, Rumania, Russia, Serbia, Spain, Sweden, Switzerland, Turkey and the USA.

The agreement that was made at the Berne meeting between these countries meant that all post could travel freely between them without any charges being imposed en route. It had taken a long time to reach this stage in the history of postal services and many previous attempts at such an agreement had floundered. But once the deal was struck, for the first time these countries could send and receive post without having to count all the items of mail to find out how much they had to pay or collect in the way of international charges.

On 18 May, 1878, the name of this international organization was changed to the Universal Postal Union (UPU). And at the same time it was decided by the members that all other countries should be encouraged to join. By the turn of the century, the majority of countries had become members of UPU.

There have been various improvements and changes in this century, and the UPU still holds the same important position today as it did when it was first founded.

ABOVE AND RIGHT In 1949 a set of stamps was issued by the British Colonies to celebrate the 75th anniversary of the Universal Postal Union. The same designs were used in different countries, a process known as omnibus.

HANDLING STAMPS

• • • •

BELOW *Trains on stamps make an attractive thematic collection, which includes an interesting example from New Zealand with a colour missing.*

The basic skills of handling stamps should become automatic, so that there is no danger of damaging stamps by picking them up clumsily. Being small and difficult to handle, they are easily damaged, so one of the first rules of stamp collecting is to learn how to handle them. It is best to use tweezers whenever possible. They may seem a little awkward at first but using them will soon become second nature if you take the trouble to master the technique.

Using tweezers

Using tweezers at all times will prevent your stamps front getting dirty and avoid fingerprint marks on the gum of mint stamps. Eventually you will find that it is much easier and quicker to sort stamps using tweezers. The best tweezers are those made of metal and with round ends. Make sure that there are no small bits of metal sticking out at the open end. You do not need much pressure to hold a stamp firmly.

Hold the tweezers about halfway along their length, not too near either end. To pick up a stamp, slide the lower lip of the tweezers under it. Until you are used to using tweezers, prevent the stamp from sliding away by gently steadying it with one finger of your other hand. Close the tweezers gently on the stamp so that you can lift it. Do not squeeze too hard.

Keeping stamps safe

Keep stamps in albums or stock books. Take particular care to avoid creasing the corners when placing stamps in a stock book and do not cram too many together. They can be kept safely sorted into packets, but take care when looking through to avoid damaging them. Do not rummage through looking for particular stamps – instead turn them out to see what is there.

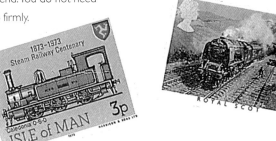

Removing backing paper

Most stamps are printed with durable inks and can be removed from backing paper by immersing them in tepid water. But, some inks and coatings react with water, so these stamps have to be 'floated off'.

Fill a bowl or sink with water. Put in all the stamps and gently stir them so they do not stick together. After about half an hour they will come off their backing and sink to the bottom. If any stamps remain attached, bend the backing paper so that a corner is free. Hold this corner gently and continue to bend off the backing paper.

Lightly press the stamps between two sheets of blotting paper. Let them dry thoroughly and keep them pressed flat under a book.

Be careful with stamps that are stuck on coloured envelopes, because the colour from the envelope often runs. It is very difficult to remove stamps from such paper without staining them. Treat these stamps separately to avoid discolouring others.

If you are not sure that the inks on the stamp are water resistant, instead of soaking the stamps carefully float the stamps, face up, on the surface of the water. The time it

1 Cut neatly around the stamp.

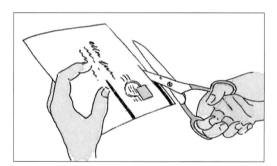

2 Float the stamps face up in a bowl of clean, tepid water for about 20-30 minutes

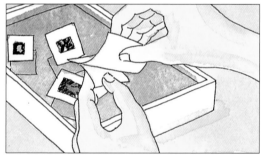

3 Use your fingers to peel the paper from the stamp (not the other way around).

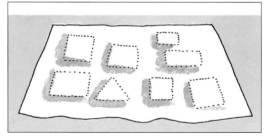

4 Dry the stamps between two sheets of blotting paper.

takes for the water to soak through the backing will depend on the type of paper, but several should be ready after 20–30 minutes.

Lift the stamp and backing paper from the surface of the water, taking care to prevent any drips from falling on to other stamps. Bend the backing paper away from the stamp until a corner of the stamp is free. Hold this corner and gently bend away the rest of the backing paper. If the gum is still stuck too firmly for you to be sure of removing the stamp without tearing it, set it aside until all the other stamps have floated off properly. Then carefully, float the half-stuck ones again.

Place the stamps face down on blotting paper. There will still be traces of gum on the back. Remove the gum by, brushing it off with a fine, clean paintbrush and water, then place a second sheet of blotting paper on top. Alternatively, just leave the stamps to dry face down on one sheet of blotting paper. This method leaves the stamps badly curled but they will soon flatten out when pressed in a stock book.

Remove stamps that require extra special care by placing them on a wet flannel or a pad of wet kitchen paper, in a saucer.

> *D*o not wrap elastic bands around bundles of stamps or clip them together with paper clips. Both of these storage methods can easily damage the stamps.

ABOVE A Morely Bright watermark detector shows the impression of the watermark on the plastic-sealed inkpad on the right-hand side.

Watermark detectors

The simplest way of looking at the watermark on a stamp is either to hold the stamp to the light or to place it face down on a dark surface. A number of detectors will help to show watermarks which are difficult to see.

The Morely Bright detector works on the principle that the paper is thinner at the watermark. A thin, sealed plastic sachet containing dark ink is placed over the stamp and pressure is applied evenly over it. The ink spreads but remains most dense where the paper thins on the watermark, and the impression of the watermark shows up.

A sinoscope is an expensive piece of equipment which works on the same principle as the Morely Bright detector. The stamp is placed between two plates which are held together under pressure and a light is shone on to the stamp, highlighting the watermark.

Lighter fluid will show up the watermark and any imperfections. Place the stamp face down in a small black or dark-coloured tray, or a sturdy lid from a jar. Squirt just enough lighter fuel over the stamp to cover it. Hold the stamp with tweezers and blow on it until it is dry.

Older types of detector used coloured filters to pick up watermarks, but they were not very successful and are not easy to find today.

Magnifying glass

A magnifying glass is often thought of as an essential piece of equipment for stamp collectors, second only to a pair of tweezers. This is not really true, however, espe-

cially for beginners. A magnifying glass is not an essential piece of equipment for a beginner but if you do decide that you need one, there is no point in buying a cheap glass which may give a distorted image. It is better to wait and to buy one of reasonable quality.

Consider what you might need a magnifying glass for before deciding to buy one. Perhaps if you have developed a particular interest in the smaller details that appear on some stamps, a magnifying glass will be a worthwhile investment. Sometimes, for example, there are small figures or numbers included in the design of the stamp. These show which printing plate the stamp came from. The best-known stamps with these numbers are the British penny plate number stamps issued between 1858 and 1879. On these stamps the plate number is engraved in each margin of the design. Many of the numbers can be read with the naked eye but some are quite difficult to see, so a magnifying glass is needed.

Some collectors also like to look for minor printing varieties – flaws or dots – which are repeated on sheets of stamps. These are called 'fly, speck' varieties and can be found listed in specialized catalogues. As they are very small a magnifying glass is used to spot them. Professional stamp valuers use them to look for signs of forgery or repairs.

There is a wide choice of magnifying glasses available and it is worth visiting several shops and trying out a few different sizes and magnifications.

Measuring perforations

Perforations around stamps allow them to be easily torn from a sheet. The holes need to be just the right distance apart. Too close and the sheets will tear too easily, too far apart and individual stamps may tear when they are being removed from the sheet. A set of stamps may have been issued with more than one size of per-

> *U*se a container such as a box file, a small stout box (for example an old shoe box) or a large zip plastic folder to keep your stamp collecting equipment together.

foration if different perforating machines were used. For example, if different printing companies have been used or if a machine broke down.

Perforations are measured by the number of holes in 2cm. There are two basic types of perforation gauge. The first has a selection of differently spaced dots printed on a card or plastic surface within a 2cm measure. The stamp is placed on the measure and the perforations are compared to the dots to find the best fit.

The second type of perforation gauge has a grid of lines printed on a clear plastic rule. These lines are graduated in terms of the distance between them. The rule is placed over the stamp and moved until the lines on the gauge exactly match the perforation points on the stamp. The measure is then read at the side of the scale.

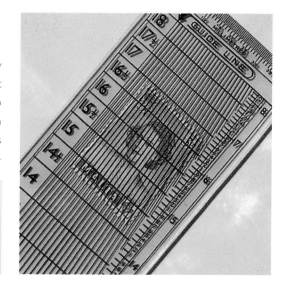

LEFT When the teeth of the stamp fall exactly on the lines of the gauge the perforation measurement can be read off the gauge on the left.

Checking the colour

Sometimes the same stamp is listed in a catalogue with more than one shade. It may be difficult to relate the colours listed to the stamp that you are examining, especially if you have only one stamp as an example. A colour guide, or colour key, shows patches (or swatches) of the basic colour types on a card, and can be matched to a stamp to decide on the exact shade which was used in the printing process.

When examining stamps for colour and using a colour key make sure that you are sitting in a good light. It is best to sit near a window in daylight, but away from direct sunlight. Artificial light is not ideal for checking colours as it can distort the true colour of the stamp.

Place the stamp on a clean piece of white paper. Hold the colour guide so that it overlaps the stamp slightly. Compare two or three shades until you find the closest match.

RIGHT A colour key shows a wide range of colour shades to match against stamps.

CHAPTER TWO

STAMP ALBUMS

• • • •

To keep your stamps in good condition on a permanent basis, you must protect them from damage. Also, part of the enjoyment of collecting anything is to be able to arrange and display the items. This applies to stamps as much as to anything else, and you need an album to exhibit your collection.

A proper album helps the philatelist to organize stamps neatly. Once they are placed in an album it is easy to see exactly what the collection contains or which other stamps you would like to add. A printed album also gives some information about the stamps on each page.

Printed all-world albums usually have fixed pages printed with large squares in which to place your stamps. They also have some illustrations of typical stamps from each country. This type of album is ideal for the new collector.

One-country albums are particularly suitable if you decide to specialize by collecting the stamps of only one country. The pages are also printed with squares and helpful illustrations but they are loose-leaf so that pages may be moved. The printed squares do not cover the page completely in this type of album. Instead, they are grouped so that sets of stamps from the country are shown together. The value and description of each stamp may be printed near the empty square. Each year new blank pages are published for this type of album to hold current stamps or extra items which you have collected. You will find this album very useful if you want to collect just one example of each stamp issued by a particular country.

LEFT Printed albums are ideal for the new stamp collector.

Blank albums have pages printed with a faint background grid of small squares to help arrange the stamps. They are made up of loose leaves so that the positions of pages can be changed or new pages added. The format is very useful for a general collection.

BELOW Spring-back blank albums are popular because they are not too expensive and they hold a good number of pages.

Stamps may have to be sorted before they can be mounted in an album. Most collectors also keep duplicates ready to swap. A stock book is ideal for both pur-

poses. Made up of stiff pages, each with a series of plastic strips which are open at the top, a stock book holds stamps neatly in place. Stock books come in a range of sizes. Not only will a stock book protect the stamps, but you will be able to quickly check which spares you have.

Mounting stamps

Specially made stamp hinges are the best method of mounting stamps in an album. They are cheap so do not be tempted to make do with adhesive tape or glue which will ruin your collection. Some stamp hinges are now produced with peelable gum, which means you can easily remove a mounted stamp. They are also available ready folded for convenience.

If you make a mistake when mounting a stamp with a non-peelable hinge, do not remove the stamp straight away – leave it for at least half an hour, until the gum is completely dry. Then it will peel off the page without damaging the stamp.

LEFT Pegfitting blank albums tend to be among the most expensive and high quality available.

RIGHT Ring albums have the advantage of lying flat when they are opened. But handle a ring album carefully because the pages have a tendency to tear around the holes.

Plastic mounts

The modern trend is to keep unused stamps with their gum untouched by a hinge – they are known as unmounted stamps. Plastic mounts are used to display unmounted stamps. These are much more expensive than hinges and are sold either in strips or cut to size. If most of the stamps in a collection are similar in size, then mounts which are already cut to the correct size are convenient. But you will probably need some strip mounts for stamps that are an unusual shape or size. Because it is difficult to cut these mounts neatly with a pair of scissors, it is best to buy a mount guillotine.

Plastic mounts are good for a specialized collection where there are fewer stamps mounted on each page, but are not suitable for a general collection in which all the stamps are placed side by side. They look very cumbersome in these arrangements and also tend to distract attention from the stamps.

If you have a valuable stamp to which you do not want to attach a hinge, it is better to keep it separate from the main collection until you have a suitable album in which to display it.

Decide on the correct position to fix the mount in the album. Remove the stamp front the mount, then lick the bottom of the mount. It is important to remove the stamp before licking the back because any moisture which finds its way between the two pieces of plastic can affect the gum on the stamp. This will leave areas of the gum highly glazed and reduce the value of the stamp. Moisten only the bottom 4 or 5mm of the mount, as this makes it easier to make any, small, final adjustments to its position.

Use tweezers to place the bottom edge of the mount in exactly the right position. Then press the mount down firmly in place. If you need to replace the mount, it will be possible to remove it from the album page without much damage.

LEFT Plastic mounts keep the gum on unused stamps in pristine condition. They are often known as Hawid or Prinz mounts after the two main manufacturers.

BELOW Hinges are the most popular and economical way to mount stamps.

Arranging stamps in an album

The first step in building up a good album is to sort all your stamps and decide how you want to display them. At first most collectors sort their stamps by country. But it is possible to rearrange the stamps several times in different ways.

Work out how to group the stamps on the pages. Do not simply start at the top left and work across and down the page, as this will only show the order in which the stamps were collected. Instead, group similar stamps together; for example, place definitives at the top and the commemoratives below.

Try not to include damaged stamps or those with heavy postmarks. But if they are important to the collection, put them in position until you find a better example.

Separate the used stamps from those that are unused. When displaying different stamps from the same set, arrange them in order according to their value.

However they are organized, stamps should be mounted carefully, in neat, straight lines. They should sit squarely on the page and not overlap their neighbours Leave gaps if necessary, to separate groups of stamps or to allow you to insert stamps in the future.

When you have more than one example of the same stamp, select the best one for your collection. This means choosing an undamaged stamp with the neatest postmark. Set other duplicates aside in your swap book.

If you do not want to put sorted stamps straight into your album, find some clean envelopes. Label them clearly and keep the stamps inside.

RIGHT Tweezers are an essential piece of equipment when handling stamps. There are several different designs to choose from.

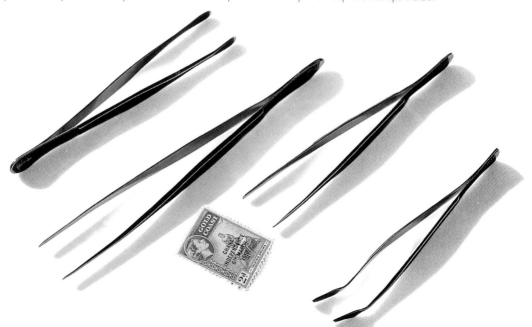

CHAPTER THREE

WHAT IS IN A STAMP?

• • • •

As the collection grows it becomes important to understand something about the way in which stamps are made, why they are used, and the journeys they make. If you take a close look at any stamp it will reveal a lot about itself.

Used and unused stamps

Stamps which are saved off letters, parcels and packets and have a postmark are 'used'. Stamps bought from a post office which have not been postmarked are

REPUBLIK

3.50 S
DÜRER

KUNST SCHÄTZE

ÖSTERREICH

A. PILCH   1971   R. TOTH

Face value

Country name

Designer's name   Postmark   Printer's name

Congratulations

EïR   JULY 23rd 1986

15P   ISLE OF MAN

C. CORLETT   1986   BDT

Perforations

Reason for issue

HRH PRINCE ANDREW & MISS SARAH FERGUSON

Face value   Year of issue   Country of issue

ABOVE From left to right, stamps from: China, North Korea, Taiwan and Japan.

unused stamps and are said to be in mint condition. It is not good practice to mix unused and used stamps randomly in a collection. Some collectors are particularly interested in stamp design, so they do not want used items with the designs partly hidden by a postmark. Others prefer stamps with postmarks, to show where the stamps have been.

Stamps which appear to be used, with neat postmarks but which still have the gum untouched have been postmarked by the postal authority, then sold at a discount to collectors. These 'cancelled to order' stamps are the same as those used to post letters, but it is better to have a genuine used example.

Some countries produce dummy stamps called appendix issues. The 'postmark' is included as part of the printing process and they usually have all of their gum on the back. They should not be included in your collection.

Postmarks

Postmarks prevent stamps being used again and provide a record of when and where a letter was posted. There are three main types of postmark.

A circular date stamp (s.d.s) is a circular post mark which shows the date of posting. It is applied by hand and includes the name of the town or city around the outside. The date, and sometimes time of posting, are in the centre. These are the most prized of the postmarks.

Sometimes special-event postmarks are used, most commonly for cancelling first-day covers, and these include many elaborate designs. These postmarks are made up of a circular date stamp with the design or message to one side. They are the most common type because they are used in automatic cancelling machines. These postmarks often obliterate much of the stamp and they can look ugly; avoid having them in a collection.

Parcel cancels are the heaviest postmarks used. They are designed to cancel several stamps at once and to work on difficult surfaces. The stamps are obscured so much that they are not worth collecting.

Country of origin

In recognition of the fact that Great Britain was the first country to issue postage stamps it is the only country allowed to issue stamps without a name or initials, but showing only the head of the Queen instead. However, before international postal regulations were generally accepted, quite a few countries printed stamps without names or other means of identification on them.

Stamps with no name or initials are not particularly common and it is usually not difficult to identify the origin of a stamp. Stamps from countries which use completely unfamiliar alphabets can be difficult to identify at first, but once you have collected a good batch of foreign stamps you will soon learn to recognize the names of the main countries. Check any unfamiliar names in the list on page 36.

Occasionally, two countries get together and cooperate to issue the same design on stamps. This is often to celebrate a particular event, for example, for the Australian bicentenary, both Britain and Australia printed stamps which were based on the same design.

ABOVE Australia and Britain teamed up to produce a joint issue (stamps based on the same design) to celebrate the Australian bicentenary.

Year of issue

An increasing number of countries include the year of issue at the bottom of the stamp. If the year is not given, you may be able to decide the year that the stamp was issued by other clues, such as the design – for example if it marks a centenary or other special occasion.

Knowing the year of issue can be very useful for organizing the stamps in chronological order in your album. It also helps if you are trying to find information about them in a stamp catalogue.

Face value

Face value is the term used for the value of the stamp, usually the price printed on it. This is nearly always printed in figures and is therefore easy to read and understand. A few stamps from the Middle East have their values printed in Arabic figures.

Usually the currency is also indicated, although some modern designs have abandoned the currency symbol. The majority of countries have changed their currencies at least once since they started issuing stamps and it is interesting to find examples of different currencies.

Printers and designers

The names of the printers and artists or designers are sometimes included underneath the design on face of the stamp.

BELOW Some companies overprinted their names on stamps to prevent them being stolen.

COMMEMORATIVE AND DEFINITIVE STAMPS

Definitive stamps are the regular-issue stamps of a country, the ones that will be used for a number of years. They may either be small stamps, often showing the leader of the country, or they may be larger and pictorial. A pictorial issue (or group) of definitives usually consists of stamps with a similar design, showing aspects of a theme related to the country. For example, sets of stamps may feature buildings or wildlife. Definitive stamps have to cover all the postal rates, so their face value ranges from the smallest unit of currency to high-value stamps for use on large parcels.

BELOW Definitive stamps from a selection of countries.

ABOVE Commemorative stamps from a range of countries.

Commemorative stamps are produced to mark important events or anniversaries. They are usually larger and more colourful than definitive stamps and the reason for issuing the set will be shown quite clearly in the design. Commemorative sets are often made up of between two and six stamps of different face values, although there are exceptions when just one or two values may be printed. As well as sheets of stamps, commemoratives are sometimes printed in blocks of sets, each surrounded by a margin, rather like a miniature sheet of stamps. These are produced especially for stamp collectors.

Paper

High quality, fine smooth paper is required for printing the detail found on stamps. Paper production is a complex and precise process, which is now mainly done by machine. The paper affects the quality of the printing. Modern paper coatings can be recognized by the sharp quality of the printing.

Vegetable fibre (mainly wood) and rags, including linen and cotton are pulped. The pulp is refined and improved by the addition of whitener, resin or size (gelatinous glues), clay, chalk or minerals. The ingredients added determine the type of paper. Phosphorescent materials which are required to activate automatic sorting machines are also added at this stage.

The mixture is then drained on a conveyor belt system and rolled by machine. The paper passes over the rollers (called dandy rollers) while it is still wet and the rollers compress the sheets and mark a pattern, or watermark, on the paper.

The two main types of paper used to print stamps are 'wove' and 'laid' paper. Wove paper has a woven mark running through it, produced by passing the paper over rolls which are covered in a mesh of wire in a woven pattern, similar to cloth.

Most old stamps are printed on wove paper. If you hold an old stamp up to the light, then turn it slightly until it is at the correct angle to see the texture of the paper,

LEFT The stamp printed on coated paper (left) has much sharper printing than the one on uncoated paper (right).

you will just be able to see a plain, even woven pattern. This is similar to the pattern in the paper used for printing newspapers.

Laid paper has a pattern, or watermark, of parallel lines running close together through it. You will also find them in high-quality writing paper.

Four other types, though uncommon, should be mentioned just in case you come across them:

Chalky paper was used until recently. It is coated before being used. This gives the stamp a shiny surface and the printing is much sharper.

Granite paper is sometimes found on stamps issued at the beginning of the century. It is a wove paper which also has coloured fibres in it. These fibres are easily visible on the back of the stamp.

Batonne paper has a pattern of parallel lines set some distance apart running through it.

Quadrillé paper has a pattern of lines set in squares.

MAKING PERFORATIONS

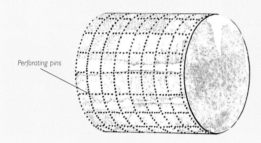

Perforating pins

Comb punch

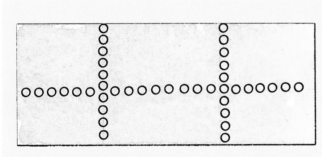

Comb perforations

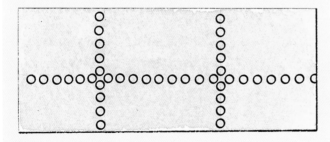

Line perforations

Watermarks

The watermark pattern is pressed into the paper when it is made by small metal stamps known as 'bits' attached to the rollers. The paper is slightly thinner in the watermark area and the impression can usually be seen by holding the stamp up to the light (see page 13).

Watermarks were originally intended to make stamps more difficult to forge. Today's advanced printing methods mean that realistic forgeries are difficult to make, so watermarks are no longer as important. Many countries have stopped using them.

A great variety of watermark designs have been used the world over – crowns, anchors, orbs, national emblems and royal cyphers (Britain), an elephant's head (India), a swan (Western Australia), a lion (Norway), turtles (Tonga), a pineapple (Jamaica), a shell (Travancore), horn (Norway and Holland), Bastito hats (Lesotho) plus numerous emblems, stars, letters and numbers.

Gum

Until the late 1960s gum arabic was normally used on stamps. However, this shiny gum gave the stamps a tendency to curl, or discolour, and to stick together, especially in hot and humid conditions. Synthetic gums are now used, the most common being polyvinyl alcohol (PVA), which has a matt surface and is almost invisible. A tinge of yellow is often added to make the gum slightly visible on the stamps.

Self-adhesive stamps have been produced by several countries including Gibraltar, Sierra Leone and Tonga. These are sold on backing paper which is peeled off before the stamps are fixed to envelopes.

Perforations

When the first stamps were issued they did not have perforations. Instead they had to be cut from the sheet with a pair of scissors. This was an inconvenient and time-consuming process. In the early years of stamp production which followed there were numerous experiments aimed at developing a way of easily separating single stamps from sheets.

Eventually in the 1850s, Henry Archer invented a machine which made lines of holes around each stamp. He sold the patent for his perforating machine to the British Government and the first sheets of fully perforated stamps were put on sale in 1854.

There are two main types of perforation. They are known as comb and line perforations. They are made by two sets of sharp pins mounted on a drum which pierce the paper from above and below. You may also come across pin perforations and roulettes.

The best postmarks to collect are the neatest, usually the ones with a circular datestamp. However, the ideal postmark need not be the one which falls just across the corner of the stamp. Some collectors like to see as much of the postmark as possible to show that the stamp was used at the correct time for its date of issue. In fact in some collections the ideal used stamp is one which has a light postmark perfectly centred on the stamp – commonly referred to as 'socked on the nose'.

Comb perforations are punched into the paper after the stamps have been printed. Modern perforating machines punch the horizontal and vertical holes at the same time. The perforations form a regular pattern around the stamps.

Older stamps had the horizontal and vertical perforations punched in two separate operations. These are called line perforations and they can be recognized by the fact the holes do not match perfectly at the corners of the stamp. Instead of having perforations punched out, the holes were made by machines which had only one set of sharp pins. The perforation marks are stamped from above but no paper is removed.

Roulettes

Roulettes are cuts made between the stamps. They do not go right through the paper and none of the paper is removed. The most common roulette has small, straight cuts around the frame of the stamp.

Sometimes the roulette teeth are inked by the printers and the stamps are said to be rouletted in colour. Other roulettes include a zigzag made up of short straight cuts marked at an angle in alternate directions. A serpentine roulette has the cuts marked in undulating wavy lines.

STAMPS IN THE MAKING

The first stage in producing a new stamp is to commission an artist to create a new design. The artist paints the picture to be used on the stamps in an enlarged form – usually about 15cm (6in) square for square stamps. Reaching the final piece of colour artwork means going through many official decisions. Even when the design has finally been approved, this is only the beginning of the printing process.

The final, approved colour artwork is put through a special machine which produces a separate photographic image of each colour used in the design (usually four). This process is known as colour separation.

Each of these colour images is then repeated side by side to make up a

sheet. Each proof is printed in one colour only. The proofs for each colour are checked for strength of colour and accuracy.

Each separate colour sheet is produced in the form of a fine screen which breaks the pattern into the tiny dots. This pattern of dots is etched on a copper printing

LEFT This artist's painting was a design for the new stamp to be issued for the Silver Jubilee of King George V of England in 1935. This one was drawn actual size, but complicated pictures are often drawn larger at this stage.

ABOVE AND RIGHT A die proof was an engraving of a design for printing on stamps produced by older methods. A proof would be printed from the finished engraving before the go-ahead was given for the stamps. This die proof

would be checked carefully for errors in the engraving. These are typical die proofs for a New Brunswick shining stamp (1851) and one for a US Sanitary Fair stamp.

cylinder. The colours are then recombined to recreate the artist's original design in the modern printing processes

To print the stamps, ink is spread over the cylinders (one colour per cylinder) and the surface is wiped before the design is transferred to the paper, one colour at a time. The paper may pass through several different colour cylinders to complete the design of the stamp. This is similar to the recess printing method except that the etched dots are very shallow.

The machines print the sheets of stamps on large rolls of gummed paper, so that once the colour plates are set up the process can run off the stamps very quickly.

ABOVE Colour trials were samples used to decide on the actual colours which would be printed for each value of stamp in a set made up of the same design. These were examined and discussed by officials. Here are three examples of King Edward VII stamps, used in Kenya, Uganda and Tanganyika while they were known collectively as 'British Central Africa'. The centre trial was chosen for the 1a value but the others were not used.

BELOW These samples show colour proofs for a set of stamps. Each proof is printed in one colour only.

Printing methods

Printing the first stamps was a skillful, very slow process in which the design was first engraved by hand on a special steel plate. Many of the stages have now been automated and computerized, but it is worth knowing about the different methods which have been used in the past and today so that they can be recognized when examining stamps.

There are five basic methods of printing. Photogravure (see page 28) is the most usual method that is used today because it is ideal for creating the detailed and multicoloured designs that are used on modern stamps. It also has the advantages of being fast and cheap.

When stamps printed by the photogravure method are viewed under a strong magnifying glass the design is made up of many small, coloured dots.

In the process of line-engraved or recess printing the design is cut, engraved or 'recessed' into a metal plate known as the printing plate. The plate is covered with

ABOVE Some German propoganda forgeries.

ink, then the surface is wiped clean, leaving the ink in the recesses. The plate is then applied under pressure to slightly dampened paper to ensure that the ink makes the best impression.

Stamps printed using the recess printing method are easy to recognize because the printed area is made up of fine lines of ink which stand out from the paper. You may even be able to feel the tiny ridges by carefully running the tip of one finger over the surface of the paper, but this is not always possible.

Recess printing is a relatively expensive method of printing and it is limited to the use of one or two colours. It is no longer widely used.

Typographed printing dominated stamp production from the 1850s until the 1930s. It is the opposite of recessed printing. The design is raised above the surface of the printing plate. Rollers coated in ink are used to apply the ink to this raised surface. The design is then transferred to the paper by stamping it on.

If you look carefully at the back of an unused stamp that has been printed using this method, you should be able to make out small ridges, especially around the edges of the design.

In lithographed printing a flat printing plate is used and its surface is treated with special chemicals to create the shape of the design. The chemicals ensure that the ink only sticks to areas of the design to be printed.

Offset lithography is a modern development of this printing technique. For this method the image is transferred from the plate to a rubber roller before being printed on the paper.

Embossed printing

The paper on which the stamps are printed is sandwiched between two plates. The design is recessed on one plate and raised on the other. This method is very slow and expensive, and is therefore rarely used. However, it was used for some stamped postal stationery until quite recently.

In a modern variation of embossing, called blind embossing, only the raised plate is used to highlight certain features in the stamp design.

Phosphor

There were a number of experiments in the late 1950s to try to develop a machine which would automatically sort envelopes so that the addressed side was uppermost. Having envelopes the right way up means that the postage stamps can be cancelled automatically and the mail is sorted more quickly. These machines are known as automatic letter facing machines.

One of the most successful machines used phosphorescent ink, which gives off a small amount of visible light for some time after being exposed to ultraviolet light. The ink was applied in bands to the sides of the stamps and these bands are known as phosphor lines. As mail went through the machine, it would recognize the phosphor lines on stamps and turn the envelope with that side facing up.

Phosphor bands are not always easy to see, especially on used stamps. But if you hold the stamp up and tilt it at an angle so that light is reflected off the surface, you may notice that the phosphor lines are matt while the rest of the surface is shiny.

Recently stamps with phosphor bands have been replaced by others whose surface is completely covered with a phosphor ink. Alternatively, the phosphor may be included in the paper or the coating.

ABOVE A thematic collection featuring ships on stamps.

Before phosphor stamps were introduced in Great Britain, experiments were done using black lines of material which conducted electricity. These thin vertical lines printed on the backs of stamps are known as graphite lines. They may be found on low-value stamps issued in 1957.

Errors and varieties

Sometimes mistakes occur at the very first stage of making a stamp, when the artist draws the first design. Despite the fact that the picture on each stamp must be checked and approved many times before it ever reaches the printer, some errors have slipped through. These stamps are fairly common as the error may well not be corrected in later printings. Sometimes it may be corrected when the stamp reprints, in which case it is a good idea to have an example of the 'before' and 'after' stamps in your collection.

With new stamps being printed in such large numbers it is not surprising that there are occasional misprints. Although the printers take great care to ensure that all the sheets with printing errors are destroyed, a few do pass through all the checking stages and are released to the Post Office without being noticed.

The most valuable errors are stamps with missing colours or without perforations. Not only are these the most striking, but they are usually very scarce.

Other varieties are sometimes caused when the paper is folded before going into the perforating machine, or at a join in the paper where a new roll was started during the printing. Occasionally there may be a missing phosphor mark or other coating.

Doctor blade flaws are caused when the blade (known as the doctor blade) which wipes the ink off the printing plate makes a mistake. This results in bands of colour running down the sheet.

There are also numerous minor varieties which occur when the printing plate is made. These are known as constant varieties by collectors because they are found in the same place in every sheet.

DESIGN ERRORS

ABOVE On this stamp from the town name, Jesselton, is spelled incorrectly as 'Jessleton'.

ABOVE The boat on this Fiji 1½d stamp is unmanned. This design error was later corrected.

ABOVE Christopher Columbus with a telescope which had not been invented in his lifetime.

CHAPTER FOUR

BUYING STAMPS

• • • •

The first stamps in your collection will probably be off the mail received by family and friends. So make sure that they do not get thrown away by mistake. Let as many friends and relatives as you can know that you are collecting and ask them to save all their stamps for you, especially those from overseas. Aim to collect as many stamps as you can find, from as many different countries as possible.

It is also a good idea to invest in a large packet of all-world stamps in order to get your collection off to a good start. Choose the biggest and most varied selection you can afford. Look out for these packets in stamp shops, stationers or newsagents. If the shops do not have anything to offer, buy a stamp magazine and read through the advertisements where you will almost certainly come across packs of all-world stamps to purchase by mail order.

If you have time, it can be a valuable exercise, as well as an interesting one, to look through what stamps are on offer and to decide which ones best fit into your collection. Discovering the scope of philately early on will help to highlight any specialized areas that you particularly enjoy and would like to concentrate on.

You will find a wide variety of packets in the shops. They may contain stamps from all over the world or specialize in one country. Alternatively, some packets hold stamps with a common theme. You will be able to see most, if not all, of the stamps that are included in the packet from the outside, so take time to choose the selection that interests you most.

BELOW The contents of stamp packets are visible. They often contain stamps from one country or on a particular theme.

Stamps on paper

Stamp shops sell bags containing stamps stuck to pieces of the original envelope. They are sold by weight, and are known as kiloware bags. The bags will contain duplicates which you can hold as swaps. Sometimes the bag contains some high-value stamps.

Kiloware stamps are cheaper than packets, and they are ideal for bulking up a small collection. Before a bag of kiloware stamps can be placed into your album, the stamps have to be soaked or floated off the paper, as explained on page 12.

BELOW Thematic collections can be based on wildlife.

Peacock

Starter packs

These are for the young collector who is just starting a collection. They contain some of the basic necessities such as a simple album, a packet of stamps, hinges and tweezers. Once you have become a serious collector, a starter pack is not a good choice.

Swapping

It is surprising just how quickly the stamp enthusiast builds up a small stock of duplicates. Keep the best stamps for your collection and set the others aside in a swap book to exchange for new stamps with other collectors.

New issues

Buy new stamps from the post office. Commemorative sets ought to be bought as they are issued, so it is a good idea to plan ahead and to note the dates when new stamps are to be released. The Post Office prints leaflets, sometimes with a calendar, listing dates when the new issues are due. The Post Office sells special packs of stamps with postcards and envelopes for first day covers.

Stamp shops

As your collection grows you will have more reason to buy single stamps rather than relying on finding good examples in packets. This is when a stamp shop will be useful. As well as packets, kiloware bags and albums, most shops display individual stamps. They also display pages from old collections – usually each page is individually priced. Most shops have boxes of covers for customers to look through. The main stock of stamps is stored in albums behind the counter. Ask to see stamps of the country which interests you and the dealer will be happy to help and to answer questions, even though your purchases may be small.

Mail order

Most shops offer a mail-order approval service. Stamps from a particular country or theme are mounted and priced in small books, known as approval books, which are sent to you to look through and to buy the ones you want. The approval book has to be returned along with the money for purchases. However, as you will be expected to pay for the postage both ways, as well as for the stamps bought, it can be expensive, especially for a new collector.

Stamp clubs

Ask at the local library for information on stamp clubs or philatelic societies in the area. Clubs usually have junior sections and joining one is an ideal way to meet other collectors. They are also a good place to pick up hints and tips as well as for swapping duplicates. Most clubs run an exchange packet, which is similar to the dealer's approval service except that the books are made up by club members and the stamps are often much cheaper.

Stamp clubs hold regular meetings, with displays and talks by members or invited guests. Other events taking place throughout the year usually include an auction and competitions.

Stamp dealers

Stamp dealers provide a number of services in addition to offering lists of stamps which they have for sale, and many dealers include approval services and postal auctions. Check stamp magazines for addresses and details of services.

Fairs and exhibitions

Stamp fairs are usually held in a hotel or a church hall. Dealers sell their goods at stands. Fairs are very useful for new collectors because many of the stands are run by spare-time dealers – philatelists who buy and sell stamps as a hobby and who may offer bargains.

Stamp exhibitions are usually well publicized. An entry fee is sometimes charged. Many of the more important dealers take stands and there are displays of stamps which have been entered in the competitions organized for the exhibition. Allow enough time to have a good look round and to pick up useful tips. You may be able to incorporate some of the ideas in your collection.

BELOW A kiloware bag is something of a lucky dip.

WHERE A STAMP COMES FROM

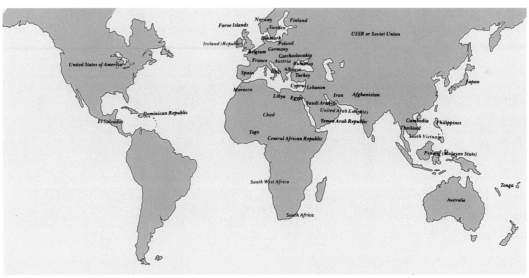

NAME ON STAMP	COUNTRY NAME	NAME ON STAMP	COUNTRY NAME	NAME ON STAMP	COUNTRY NAME
Afghanes	Afgha.istan	Helvetia	Switzerland	Sachsen	Saxony (German State)
Arabie Saoudite	Saudi Arabia	Italia	Italy	Salvador	E I Salvador
Bayern	Bavaria (German State)	Jugoslovija	Yugoslavia	Shqipëria (and similar)	Albania
België or Belgique	Belgium	Kibris	Cyprus	Siam	Thailand
Braunschweig	Brunswick (German State)	KSA	Saudi Arabia	South Africa	South Africa
Cambodge	Cambodia	LAR	Libya	South West Africa	South West Africa
CCCP	USSR or Soviet Union	Liban or Libanaise	Lebanon	Suomi	Finland
Centrafricaine	Central African Republic	Magyar Posta	Hungary	Sverige	Sweden
Ceskoslovensko	Czechoslovakia	Maroc	Morocco	SWA	South West Africa
Danmark	Denmark	Nippon	Japan	Tchad	Chad
DDR	East Germany	Norge	Norway	Toga	Tonga
Deutsche Bundespost	West Germany	Österreich	Austria	Togolaise	Togo
Berlin	West Berlin	Persia	Iran	Türkiye	Turkey
Deutsche Post or Reich	Germany	Pilipinas	Philippines	UAE	United Arab Emirates
Dominicana	Dominican Republic	Polska	Poland	UAR	Egypt or Syria
Eesti	Estonia	Pulao Pinang	Penang	USA	United States of America
Egypte, or Egyptienne	Egypt	Reichspost	Germany	Vaticane	Vatican city
Eire	Ireland (Republic)	RF	France	Viet-nam Cong Hoa	South vietnam
Espana or Espagola	Spain	Romana	Rumania	Viet-nam Dan Chu Cong Hoa	North Vietnam
Froyar	Faroe Islands	RSA	South Africa	YAR	Yemen Arab Republic
Francais	Frame	Rwandaise	Rwanda	Z. Afr. Republiek	Transvaal (South African State)
Gronland	Greenland	SA	Saudi Arabia		

Auctions

Auctions are an established way of buying and selling stamps. Stamps may be auctioned individually, in blocks, in sheets, as groups or even in boxfuls, and each is known as a 'lot'. All the lots included in the sale are described in the auction catalogue with estimated selling prices, or values as given in general stamp catalogues such as those published by Stanley Gibbons and Scott. All the lots are available for viewing before the sale and the details will be given in the auction catalogue.

Descriptions in auction catalogues vary considerably. Local sales are usually accompanied by catalogues giving only a brief description, because all the potential buyers will be present at the auction to view the lots which interest them. However, large international auction houses often sell to overseas bidders who do not have a chance to examine the stamps in person before the sale. Customers may place their bids over the telephone or by post, so details in the catalogue must be as accurate as possible.

There is a wide selection of lots on offer, from individual stamps and covers to all-world collections. As your collection develops, you may consider buying a useful auction lot of all-world stamps. Remove the ones you want for your collection, then sell the remainder again – either offer them back through the same auction house, or sell them individually.

*S*tamps sunk at sea. The 'Leaping Tiger' stamp of the Federated Malay States (Negri Sembilan, Pahang, Perak and Selangor) is well known among philatelists for its many different values and corresponding colours. A delivery delay in 1922 resulted in a shortage of 4c stamps, so 5 million 3c stamps were overprinted with a 4c value. Before these surcharged 3c stamps were put into use, new supplies of the regular 4c arrived from the printers and, apart from samples supplied to officials, all of the overprinted 3c stamps were placed in weighted boxes and sunk in the sea.

LEFT This set of maximum cards showing stamp designs by artist Ralph Steadman was produced to celebrate Halley's comet.

Frama labels

For many years post offices have been using machines to automatically dispense stamps. Multi-value machines are now used in a number of countries. These machines print the value requested by the customer on special labels, known as machine labels, automat stamps or Frama labels. The name 'Frama label' is taken from the Swiss company which produced the first of these machines, which was introduced in Switzerland in 1976.

There has been a mixed reaction among collectors to these stamps or labels. Some people are avid collectors, but the majority shun them. Frama labels are not widely used so keep any covers with them intact.

Post office services

The Post Offices in many countries produce a large range of items for collectors, including presentation packs, postcards illustrating stamps and booklets, as well as unused definitive and commemorative stamps. The main post offices in some large towns have philatelic counters selling all the stamps and items produced for the special issues front the preceding year.

If there is not a philatelic counter near your home, you can order back issues by writing to the Philatelic Bureau. You can also write to the philatelic bureaux of overseas countries to buy their new issues.

馬年郵資標籤首日封 一九九〇年二月二十一日 Year of the Horse Postage Label 21st February, 1990, First Day Cover

WORLD PHILATELIC BUREAUX

Buying new stamp issues from foreign countries is not easy. Some stamp dealers may have them on offer, but it is easier to write to the philatelic bureau of the country concerned. Some countries offer a standing-order service for philatelists, sending out each new issue of stamps when they become available. It is best to write asking for information first, then the bureau will send details of how to obtain the stamps.

AUSTRALIA
Australia Post
Australia Stamp Bulletin
Locked Bag 8
South Melbourne
Vic 3205
Australia

BRUNEI DAR USSALAM
General Post Office
Philatelic Bureau
Bandar SM Scgawan 2050
Brunei Darussalam

CHINA
China National Stamp
Corporation
Hepingmen
Beijing
China

CANADA
Philatelic Service
National Philatelic Centre
Canada Post Corporation
Antigonish
Nova Scotia B2C 2R8

CYPRUS
Philatelic Service
Department of Postal
Services
Nicosia
Cyprus

DENMARK
Postens Fimaerkecenter
Vesterbrogade 67
DK-1620 København V.
Denmark

FINLAND
P&T of Finland
Postimerkkikeskus
POB 654
SF-00101 Helsinki
Finland

FRANCE
Service Philatelique
18 rue Franfois-Bonvin
(F) 75758 PARIS cedex 15
France

GREAT BRITAIN
The British Philatelic
Bureau
Edinburgh
EH3OHN

GUERNSEY
Postal Headquarters
Guernsey
Channel Islands

HONG KONG
General Post Office
2 Connaught Place, Central
Hong Kong

ISRAEL
Ministry of
Communications
Philatelic Services
12 Yerushalayim Blvd
61080 Tel Aviv-Yafo

ITALY
Direxione Generale Post e
Telecommunication
Vendita Francubolli per
Coliezioni
1-00100 Row

JERSEY
Jersey Philatelic Bureau
PO Box 304L
St Helier
Jersey
Channel Islands

KOREA
Korean Philatelic Center
CPO Box 5122
Seoul 100-651
Republic of Korea

MACAU
Macau General Post
Office
Largo Do Senado
Macau

MALAYSIA
The Philatelic Bureau
Postal Headquarters
General Post Office
Dayabumi Complex
50670 Kuala Lumpur
Malaysia

MONACO
Office des Emissions
de Timbres-Poste
2 Avenue Saint-Michel
MC-98030 Monaco Cedex

NEW ZEALAND
Philatelic Bureau
New Zealand Post Ltd.
Private Bag
Wanganui
New Zealand

PAPUA NEW GUINEA
PNG Philatelic Bureau
PO Box I
Boroko
Papua New Guinea

RUSSIA
Mezhdunarodnaya Kniga
Moscow, Russia

SAMOA
Philatelic Bureau
Chief Post Office
Apia
Western Samoa

SINGAPORE
Singapore Philatelic Bureau
Postal Services Group
Singapore Telecom
I Killiney Road
Singapore 0923

SOLOMON ISLANDS
Philatelic Bureau
cl - GPO Honiara
Solomon Islands

SOUTH AFRICA
Phitatelic Services
Private Bag and Intersapa
Private Bag X 505
0001 Pretoria
Republic of South Africa

SWEDEN
PFA
S-105 02 Stockholm
Sweden

SWITZERLAND
PTT Philatelic Office
CH-3030 Berne
Switzerland

THAILAND
Philatelic Division
The Communications
Authority of Thailand
Chaeng Watthana Road,
Lak Si Bangkok 10002
Thailand

UNITED NATIONS
United Nations Postal
Administration
United Nations
New York NY 10017
USA
or
Administration postale
des Nations Unies a`
Gene`ve
Palais des Nations
CH-1211 Genève 10
Switzerland

UNITED STATES
U.S. Postal Service
Philatelic Sales Division
Washington D.C. 20265-
9998

ZIMBABWE
Philatelic Bureau
Posts a munications
Corporation P.O. Box 4220
Harare

USING A STAMP CATALOGUE

Stamp catalogues are price lists or guides. They are published by leading stamp dealers around the world, including Stanley Gibbons (UK), Scott (USA), Michel (Germany), Yvert & Tellier (France), and Sassone (Italy). Catalogues cover different areas of stamp collecting. The standard type is an all-world catalogue which covers the basic stamps issued by all countries. An all-world catalogue does not usually give information on variations in the stamps (different watermarks or shades of colour for example).

Main dealers in all countries publish specialized catalogues of bottle stamps as well as all-world catalogues. For example, Stanley Gibbons publish a Great Britain catalogue; Scott publish a United States catalogue; Campbell Patterson publish a New Zealand catalogue; and Seven Seas Stamps publish an Australian catalogue.

Apart from Great Britain, most are one-volume publications. The Great Britain catalogue is published in five volumes but there are less detailed versions available in one volume. In addition, Stanley Gibbons publish a series of catalogues covering all countries, each one giving more details than the all-world catalogue.

As well as providing a guide to the value of stamps, a catalogue offers a wealth of information. All catalogues include a general section about stamps, their watermarks, their perforations and other details. Always read the information on how to use the catalogue, since the layout is often a little difficult to follow, and each company has minor variations in presentation.

BELOW AND LEFT Some 13p stamps were issued in error as part of this set of Christmas stamps due to an increase in postal rates during production.

Using a catalogue

At the front of a catalogue there is an index or contents list where relevant. The contents are in A-Z order by country or in chronological order – the order in which the stamps were issued. Other systems may be used in more specialized catalogues.

To find a stamp look up the country, then look up the year of issue, and then look down the list of stamps issued in that year to find the item.

If you do not know the year of issue then look at other stamps which are illustrated from that country. Look for those with pictures of the same ruler or with a similar style of illustration.

Catalogues usually illustrate one stamp from each set or series. Once you have found the series, simply, read down the list to find the particular stamp.

There are two columns of prices printed in catalogues. The column on the left gives the price for unused stamps and the one on the right gives the price for used stamps. Remember that these prices are the selling prices of that dealer's stock and are for stamps in perfect condition.

For each issue the catalogue gives the title of the set, the date of issue and the face value of each stamp. There is often also information about watermarks, perforations, colours, printers, printing methods and designers.

BELOW An annotated catalogue entry featuring a British Christmas card series.

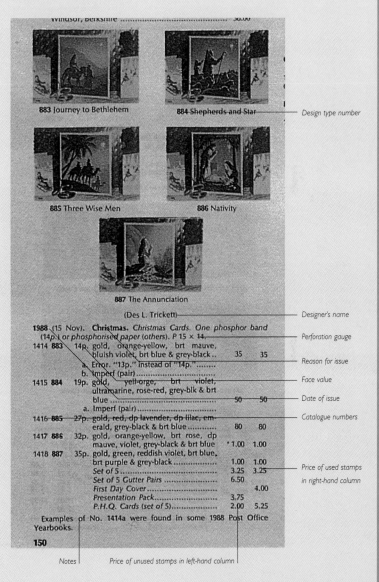

STAMPS NOT FOR POSTAGE

The majority of stamps are produced for postage purposes. Special non-postage stamps have been printed for specific purposes and they are just as interesting as the usual postage stamps, although they are not listed in stamp catalogues. Some collectors specialize in these particular stamps.

Revenue or fiscal stamps

One way in which the British Government raised revenue at one time was to require a fee to be paid on all legal documents in order to make them valid. Special stamps were stuck on to the documents to show that the correct amount had been paid. Stamps were produced for each type of document including magistrates' and other courts, and for customs and medicine duty.

The most usual use for revenue stamps was on receipts. All receipts had to have a penny stamp, which had to be signed in ink to be legal. The issue of the special receipt

stamps was phased out in Great Britain in 1881, when the ordinary penny postage stamps were inscribed 'Postage and Revenue', to enable them to be used for both purposes.

The receipt duty was at a later stage increased to twopence before being discontinued in the 1960s. You will probably see many stamps with a handwritten signature over them, or you may find the complete receipt.

Some institutions and companies which issued a large number of receipts overprinted their stamps with either the initials or the name of the company, both for the sake of convenience and in order to prevent their employees from stealing their stamps.

BELOW AND RIGHT Revenue and fiscal stamps from various countries. Clockwise from top right: Great Britain land registry; Great Britain transfer duty; Great Britain foreign bill; United States proprietary stamp;Hong Kong stamp duty; Hong Kong stamp duty; United States match duty.

Telegraph stamps

Telegraph stamps are easily distinguished because they include the word 'Telegraph'(or something very similar) on their design. Even those stamps issued by Japan used a recognizable word.

The cost of sending a telegram was paid by the customer in stamps which were then attached to a receipt.

These were discontinued at the turn of the century when ordinary stamps could be used, so all telegraph stamps are quite old.

Originally the telegraph service was run by private companies, each of which issued its own stamps. There are some interesting names, and some include the words 'Electric Telegraph' or 'Magnetic Telegraph' to emphasize the fact that the company used the latest technology.

Some telegraph offices also used special postmarks. For example, offices at racecourses had their own postmarks, such as Kempton Park Grandstand. This is a popular area of specialization in stamp collecting.

Locals

Local stamps were printed by letter delivery companies that operated independently from the Post Office, examples of which can be found from most countries. They were not valid for use outside the particular delivery company.

LEFT AND BELOW
A selection of telegraph stamps.

43

Circular Delivery Company, 1865-7: This service provided local delivery of circulars at a much cheaper rate than the Post Office.

College Stamps, 1871-94: In England there was a special delivery service which transported the mail between each of the colleges in Oxford and Cambridge.

There were a number of such services in major towns around the world, particularly in China, Germany and Sweden. Some examples are given below.

Australian Cycle Express, 1890s During the Australian gold rush cyclists pedalled through the outback in order to carry the mail from the remote gold fields to the nearest main postal link, a journey that sometimes covered over a hundred miles. By the mid-1890s camels as well as cyclists were being used to carry the post out of remote areas.

Court Bureau, 1890-1: This postal service was a special Sunday collection from London gentleman's clubs which took letters and parcels to the appropriate railway station to catch the mail train.

Shipping Lines: Various shipping lines also provided postal services linking islands and connecting mainland port towns.

ABOVE A selection of local stamps from around the world.

RIGHT AND BELOW A selection of attractive labels.

Labels

Labels were often produced to commemorate an exhibition or other special philatelic event. Some of the early designs were colourful and elaborate. Other examples are labels produced for advertising purposes and other promotions. Some labels are still used. Unfortunately many are self-adhesive and do not hold the same attraction for stamp collectors.

Railway stamps

The collecting of railway stamps is a large and sometimes specialized subject. As the railways did not interfere with the post office monopoly, letters, parcels and newspapers could be sent by train between railway stations and over

to the Post Office for the final stage of their journey if the necessary postage stamps had been applied. This was an expensive method of sending letters and parcels and it was only used when speed of delivery was a high priority. However, parcels which were collected from the station were relatively cheap to send and a similar system is still in use today, although the use of special railway stamps ceased a long time ago.

Railway stamps were used mainly during the period before the large major railway companies dominated the rail transport system, when there were many small lines. Many of the small railway lines issued their own postage stamps. The different railway company names, and the nostalgia of the age of steam trains, adds to the popularity of these stamps among collectors.

LEFT AND BELOW A selection of railway stamps.

Valuing stamps

Values given in a stamp catalogue represent the prices of stamps in perfect condition when sold by the publishers of the catalogue. Stamps which are not in absolutely perfect condition will not be sold for the catalogue price. Non professionals, especially new collectors, may well miss certain small defects which drastically reduce the value of a stamp, and which may not be obvious to collectors.

It is relatively easy, however, to arrive at an approximate value for your own collection, but there are many different factors which affect the precise figure. To value a complete collection, ignore all stamps with the minimum catalogue value which represents a handling charge and not the value of the stamp. Also ignore any that are in poor condition or forgeries. Add up the catalogue value of all the remaining stamps then divide the figure by 10.

The following are a few of the factors that reduce the value of a stamp:
• A hinge stuck on a unused stamp.
• An untidy postmark on a used example, which could halve the value.
• A creased corner or short perforation, which could mean that it is worth less than a quarter of the above value.
• A thin area, tear or other serious imperfection in the paper, which will reduce its value to about a tenth of the value of an undamaged example.

It is much more difficult to value individual stamps because so much depends on condition, where the stamp is to be sold and the demand. Assuming a stamp is in perfect condition and the market has not suddenly been flooded, the approximate selling price should be about 25 per cent of the catalogue value. If it is sold by auction, the price should be higher – about 30-40 per cent of the catalogue price.

Reprints

In order to satisfy the demand for stamps by collectors a few countries printed further supplies of some stamps from the original plates. These are called reprints.

To the experienced eye they are usually quite easy to distinguish from the originals because they were printed about 20 or 30 years later. The paper is often of much better quality, the colours are brighter and the gum is smooth and glossy. Reprints are fairly common, especially in older albums.

BELOW The condition of a stamp can affect its value. From left to right: badly cut into; large margins and neat postmark but cut into in the bottom right corner; cut close at the bottom but a good postmark; good margins but an unclear postmark; a stamp in good condition with good margins.

Unless you have handled the originals, it is easy to mistake a reprinted stamp for a genuine one. Most catalogues have notes indicating which stamps have been reprinted but unfortunately these notes are not always comprehensive. If in doubt, assume the stamp is a reprint and seek an expert opinion.

Errors and varieties

Errors and varieties are those stamps with which something has gone wrong either at the design or printing stages of production. When any of the major varieties are found they create a lot of interest in the stamp world. The most valuable ones are those on a small part of one sheet, when a row of 5-10 stamps may be the only examples which exist. With so few available, it is not surprising that they sell for large sums.

Forgeries

There are two categories of forgery: those produced to deceive the Post Office (postal forgeries) and those made to deceive collectors.

Postal Forgeries are scarce and usually fetch high prices, especially if they are found on their original envelopes. One of the most famous examples of this type of forgery was used in the telegraph office of the London Stock Exchange in 1872.

The forger printed a passable likeness of the current shilling stamp, and gave a supply to an accomplice who worked on the telegraph counter. The counter clerk then used the forged stamps on the telegrams and pocketed the money that was handed over by the customers. As long as the counter clerk's books balanced at the end of the day, nobody was to know. The telegraph receipts never left the telegraph office, except for filing, until they were destroyed.

The deception was not noticed until a famous dealer purchased a quantity of old telegram forms from the post office in 1898 and noticed some of the forgeries – 26 years after the original crime was committed.

ABOVE *This stock exchange forgery was used on a telegram form with a genuine 9d stamp.*

ABOVE *British stamps from 1962 with the blue colour missing from the upper stamp.*

LEFT *British stamps which are only partly perforated.*

ABOVE *The design was printed upside down on this Canadian commemorative stamp.*

47

Some of the older forgeries are easy to detect – they were crudely printed and postmarked. Some recent examples of this kind of reproduction have the word FACSIMILE printed on the back.

Modern forgers concentrate more on repairing or faking overprints rather than producing stamps. When forging overprints or surcharges the forger takes a genuine stamp and applies a new overprint to make it appear to be more valuable. Some forgeries are dangerously good and can fool experts. So be wary of stamps with overprints which increase their value.

Many forgeries were produced during the Second World War by the British and the Germans. The designs were usually based on the stamps used at the time.

BELOW Overprint forgeries on British stamps. Clockwise from top left: genuine overprint; lithographed forgery; forged overprint on a stamp that was issued later than the genuine use of the overprint shown; a very crude forgery; genuine overprint; a lithograph forgery with the overprint in an incorrect position.

Improvements and repairs

Be vigilant about looking out for repairs or improvements. Inspect stamps for tears which have been stuck together with a small amount of glue so that only a small mark remains.

Check the perforations. A stamp without perforations may have had a paper margin added by carefully building up a paper pulp around it, pressing and cutting it. These can be detected by close examination of the edge of the stamp. Missing corners can be rebuilt and thin areas in the paper can also be improved. Damaged perforations can be removed by carefully punching another row just inside the damaged section. This is quite common with stamps printed on thick paper and with widely spaced perforation holes. Watch out for stamps which are too small or with the perforations on one side not quite aligned properly.

Gum can be replaced or redistributed where a hinge has been removed. Or a stamp may be sweated to remove a hinge and leave the stamp looking unmounted. When the gum on a stamp has been changed some of the glue works its way into the fibres of the paper. A tell-tale sign is that the stamp may curl the wrong way. The perforations are always much stiffer and their points feel sharp.

Sometimes postmarks are faked, particularly on older stamps where the catalogue value of a used example is greater than that of an unused one.

CHAPTER FIVE

BUILDING UP A COLLECTION

● ● ● ●

As your collection grows you will find certain countries or certain types of stamp more interesting than others. At this stage, most collectors decide to concentrate on stamps from one or two countries, while at the same time continuing to collect others.

Be selective

It is important that all the stamps in your collection should be in the best possible condition. They should be clean, attractive and without faults. Check the following:

- Perforations should be complete, with no slightly shorter perforations or blunt corners. Imperforate stamps (stamps without perforations) should have large, even margins.
- Stamps should not have any thin patches in the paper or creases. Creased corner perforations which can be folded over easily should be counted as creases.
- The design should be well centred on the stamp.
- Unused stamps should be unmounted, if possible, or lightly-mounted. (Note that in most catalogues the price quoted for unused stamps issued after 1940 is for unmounted examples.)

- Used stamps should have a neat circular date stamp. Whether this is central or across a corner is a matter of personal preference.
- Covers ought to be in clean condition with good strikes (or impressions) of the postmarks.

Single country collections

Compiling a single-country collection is a quite simple way to begin. It soon results in a large collection which may be improved by becoming more specialized.

Some collectors concentrate on unused stamps and others on used stamps. Some collections combine both. It is also not unusual for a philatelist to limit a collection to one example of each stamp of one country – so blocks, strips or varieties are not included.

If the collection is going to contain one example of each stamp, a special printed album is ideal. These albums show which stamps have been issued by the country in each set, so the collector knows exactly what to look for. The information on the year of issue and face value of the stamps is all printed on the pages, so there is not usually enough space for adding extra notes.

BELOW Sports events can make an interesting thematic collection.

RIGHT AND
BELOW
An attractive
collection based
around the
popular theme of
wild animals.

Hedgehog *Erinaceus europaeus*   Hare *Lepus capensis*   Red Squirrel *Sciurus vulgaris*   Otter *Lutra lutra*   Badger *Meles meles*

Thematic collections

Collecting by country is not the only way of organizing your stamps. Many collectors find certain topics featured on stamps are particularly interesting to collect. Instead of looking for stamps from particular countries, a thematic collector seeks out stamps which illustrate a particular chosen theme. There is a wide variety of themes on which a collection may be based, such as birds, animals, flowers, sport, space transport or perhaps a less popular subject such as food and produce. There are a large number of publications devoted to thematic collecting.

The alternative approach is to collect the stamps in the sets as they were issued. They should be arranged in A-Z order according to the name of the country in which they were issued. To show off the stamps particularly well, for each country the stamps should be organized in chronological order of date of issue.

Although well-organized stamps make the collection more attractive to look at, they can cause problems with the presentation of the background information. Thematic stamp collections usually combine information about the specific stamps, with notes about the general theme.

Additions to a collection

Traditionally a collection would only contain stamps, but it is now acceptable, and more interesting, to include covers, postcards and other postal items which expand on the chosen subject. But make sure that the connection with the theme is clear.

Booklets

Booklets were first introduced at the beginning of the twentieth century. They were intended to be a convenient way of buying and carrying stamps. The first booklets were usually made up of panes of six stamps either stitched or stapled together with interleaving pages between stiff outer covers. Today booklets are simply a folded cover with a block of stamps fixed by its margin.

Many countries, such as Australia, Britain, Canada, Singapore and Sweden, produce stamp booklets, sometimes to commemorate special occasions, sometimes for permanent sale.

The booklets illustrated in this book show how the designs of booklets have changed and developed, from small, practical designs to large and exciting examples which may include labels and written information as well as stamps.

If there is space in your album, include some books in the unopened packet along with others opened out to show their contents. Use photograph corner mounts to keep them in place. Since they can take up a lot of space you may only want to show one or two. Booklet albums are available, or you can use a plain scrapbook.

LEFT AND BELOW Some examples of colourful stamp booklets from all over the world.

COLLECTING COVERS

A cover is an envelope or wrapper which has been stamped and posted. Some collectors specialize by looking for specific types of cover.

Popular covers include those which have been damaged during transit. For example, the envelope may have been ripped in a sorting machine. Some covers may have been damaged by flood or fire. Collecting crash covers is a subject in its own right, and involves covers from either airline crashes or boat wrecks. Some covers are particularly interesting, perhaps they have decorative illustrations or interesting postmarks.

First-day covers are the most readily available and probably the most popular with collectors. First-day covers are the most common. These are envelopes with a whole set of stamps on them, posted on the first day of issue. Special envelopes can be bought at a post office or from a dealer. On the day when the new set is released, a complete set is carefully stuck on to the

BELOW A typical example of a first-day cover, from Namibia.

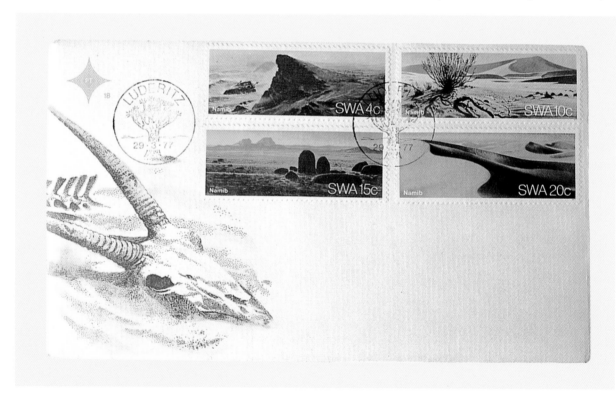

PICTURE POSTCARDS

Old picture postcards can make an interesting cover collection. The most popular subject to collect are cards which feature your home town, called topographic cards. It is always interesting to see how familiar streets and landmarks have changed over the years. Cards can also be found which show social history including any subject featuring ways of life at the time, such as farming, schools or shop fronts. Many modern cards which are collectable feature old advertising posters, and these make an ideal subject.

ABOVE AND BELOW Picture postcards
featuring an old street scene and a shop front.

LEFT A picture postcard showing
a poster reproduction.

envelope and it is posted in a special box at a post office. The stamps are cancelled with a commemorative postmark and the envelope includes a special design. A card with background information may be enclosed.

It is best to buy a special album to display covers. First-day cover albums have plastic folders instead of pages. Each folder is divided in half and has a black backing paper to display the covers to best advantage. Most are

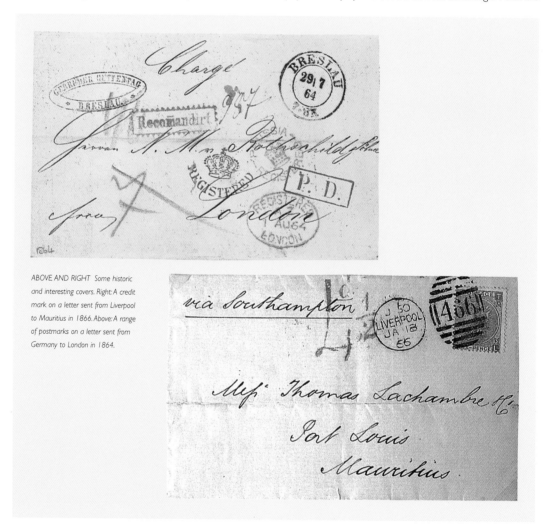

ABOVE AND RIGHT Some historic and interesting covers. Right: A credit mark on a letter sent from Liverpool to Mauritius in 1866. Above: A range of postmarks on a letter sent from Germany to London in 1864.

designed to allow four covers to be mounted on each page. There are also half-size cover albums available which hold two covers per page.

Many of the interesting markings found on old covers may still be used today, with slight changes. Look out for any cover which has an unusual postmark, hand-stamp or label applied to it. For example, you may find postage due marks; or marks giving reasons for delayed delivery; or covers which have been damaged in the post and stamped with an official mark to explain what has happened.

When collecting covers, the condition of the envelope is important and the postmark must also be good quality. It is important to distinguish between covers posted especially for collectors and those which have been used by companies or for genuine correspondence.

Because of changes in postal rates it was, and still is, often necessary to make up the correct postage with more than one stamp. Covers of this type from the nineteenth century and the beginning of the twentieth, are collectable. It is unusual to find stamps of three different values on one cover (called 'three-colour frankings'), and such covers are held in esteem by collectors.

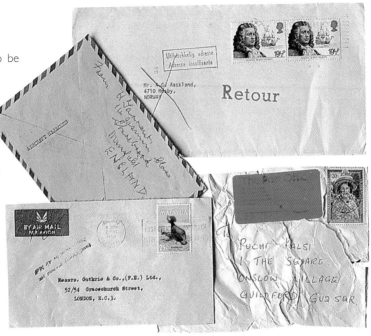

LEFT A range of collectable and interesting markings on covers include clockwise from the top: Retour (return to sender), damaged in the post, insufficient postage for transmission by Air Mail and delay due to aircraft hijacked.

Postmarks

Sometimes there is more than one postmark on a letter. The cover may have been stamped at various stages during the letter's journey and these marks are called transit marks. Other postmarks may pass on information to the post-office staff or to the person who receives the mail.

Transit marks show the route that the letter or package took from when it was posted to when it was delivered. Today, the mail usually goes straight from one place to another with only one postmark. Before the worldwide postal system was this well organized, a letter could visit several places on an international route. At each 'stop' it would be stamped. This was not just an international characteristic. Even within one country a piece of mail could pass through several offices and receive a postmark at each stage. More commonly, it received first a despatch postmark then an arrival postmark at its destination. Working out the route from some old postmarks can be quite interesting.

BELOW A set of advertising labels.

Early postmarks often did not show where they were from. Later, numbers or letters were set in parallel bars or circles then circular date stamps (see page 22) were introduced.

In the nineteenth century there were fewer post offices than there are today, so it is relatively easy to collect an example of a postmark from each post office in a particular country.

Postmarks are made by hand or by machine. In most countries ordinary mail is stamped by machine. In some small, remote places letters are still stamped by hand. Machine cancellations are usually in two parts. The first is a circular or square section with the date and town. The second is a series of wavy lines or a slogan.

Instruction marks are usually only put on mail when something is wrong. For example, a postage due mark is used if there is something to pay. When a letter has to be returned, or is misdirected instructional marks are stamped on the envelope to send it on its way again.

Advertising on covers

Postal authorities sometimes supplemented their income by selling advertising space. During the last century the advertising on covers was much more elaborate and attractive, so much so that some envelopes were covered with illustrations, leaving only a small space for the name and address. The craftsmanship of early examples has made them quite valuable now. More recent examples are simpler and are often quite reasonably priced.

Writing up a collection

In a specialized collection there are usually fewer stamps on each page and some information should be given beside the stamps. A large set of stamps can require a page on its own. Sometimes two small sets may be placed on the same page, but they should be clearly separated.

When displaying a few stamps on plain pages arrange them neatly and symmetrically and try to balance the page. It is not necessary to arrange the stamps in strict value order, although they are better done this way. Allow room for writing notes which make the page more interesting. You will probably have rows of different lengths.

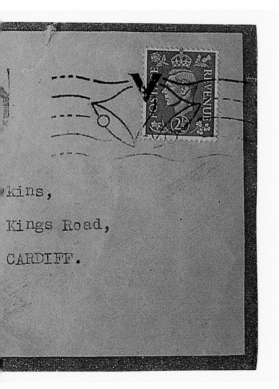

LEFT A booklet pane advertising Esso tyres.

LEFT A heavily illustrated cover advertising Kardov flour.

The written notes should be included near the relevant stamps. The information on the page should be chosen to give anyone looking at the collection a better understanding of the stamps.

It is usual to include the name of the set as a heading at the top of the page. The date of issue plus details of the watermark, perforations, printers and printing method used should be put beneath the heading, near the top of the page.

Notes about special features which appear on an individual stamp, such as an unusual shade, should be written immediately below it. Extra information about the whole set of stamps, such as the reason why the set was issued or any historical significance may be written below the stamps or at the foot of the page. However, do not get carried away with adding extra information, take care that the background information does not come to dominate the page. Bear in mind that the stamps should still be the main feature of the album.

BELOW A page from a specialized Hong Kong collection is annotated with a draughtsman's pen.

RIGHT A display of stamps from Singapore with handwritten notes.

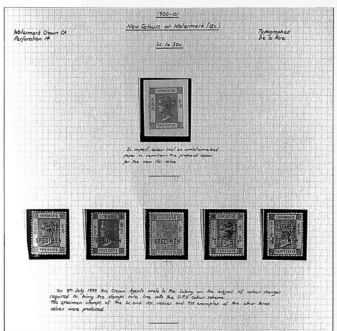

The majority of stamp collections are written up by hand using a pen and ink but there are several other ways of presenting the written information that can look equally good. Choose a pen with a fine nib. Several different types can be used – a fountain pen, a draughtsman's pen or fine-point, felt-tip. Do not use ballpoint.

All notes should be written in black. Serious philatelists frown on blue and other colours. Fine red lines can be used to underline headings.

If you do not want to write up the collection by hand you can use stencil sets or characters printed on special backing sheets ready to rub on paper, but they are expensive. Alternatively, type or print notes on blank paper, then stick them on the album page.

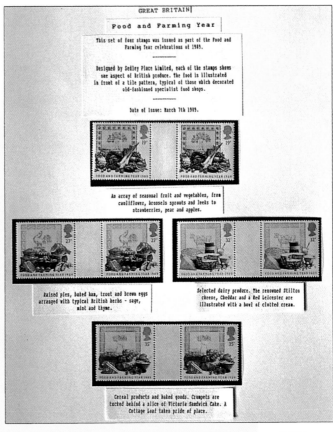

LEFT A specialized British collection with stencilled notes.

ABOVE A thematic collection about food with wordprocessed annotation.

G L O S S A R Y

• • • •

ABOVE An abnormal 8d stamp which was printed violet in error, rather than the correct orange-yellow.

Abnormal An example from a plate which was not officially issued, and is one of a few released in error.

Approvals Stamps which are sent out to collectors on a buy-or-return basis.

Bisect When they ran out of stamps of a certain value, the Post Office allowed a stamp of a higher value to be cut in half and both halves used in the normal way.

Block Four or more stamps that are still together in their original square or rectangular shape.

Booklet Pane A sheet containing only a small number of stamps made for putting in a booklet.

Cinderellas Those items which resemble postage stamps but are not official Government issue. They include revenue stamps, and telegraph stamps.

RIGHT This letter from Singapore to Glasgow bears a bisect stamp.

Classic The initial issue of stamps produced by those countries which first used postage stamps.

Colour Changeling A stamp which has had its colour changed by exposure to water or sunlight.

Colour Trial In recess and typograph printing the design is prepared first. Once the engraved die has been approved the correct colours need to be chosen. Usually one of the dies is printed in a range of colours which are then sent off for approval.

Commercial Cover Usually commercial letters. Ordinary correspondence can also be classified as commercial in order to distinguish it from philatelic covers.

Cover The outer covering of any item sent by post. This may be an envelope or a wrapper.

Cylinder Number Each printing cylinder is given a number and this is printed in the margin of the sheet of stamps.

Die Proof A printed impression taken from the die in order to check for any small defects in the engraving or to be sent to the postal authorities for their final approval before the stamps are printed.

Doctor Blade A blade that removes surplus ink from the printing cylinder. If the printing stops at all then parallel lines of ink, called doctor blade flaws, are left each side of the spot where the blade was touching the cylinder. These two lines of colour can be quite spectacular and are highly collectable.

Dry Print If the ink in one of the printing cylinders runs very low, less ink is transferred to the printing plate.

Fancy Cancel Some illustrated postmarks used in the United States between 1850 and 1900.

First-Day Cover This is a cover bearing a stamp (or a set of stamps) that was posted on the day of issue. The post office issues special first day covers for each new stamp issue.

Fly Specks Minor errors created when the designs are laid out on the printing cylinder and repeated in the same position on each sheet.

Gutter Margins Sometimes sheets of stamps are issued in one or more panes. The margin between these panes is the gutter margin.

Imperforate A stamp issued without any perforations is said to be imperforate

BELOW Dry prints are exemplified in this block of British 9d stamps.

LEFT A doctor blade flaw can be seen down the right hand side of this block of British George VI 6d stamps.

Imprimatur British Victorian stamps which have been cut from imperforate sheets stored at the post office. One sheet of each value and different plate number was kept for archive and reference purposes.

Key Plate From the 1890s and 1930s some of the colonial powers used the same design of stamp in several colonies. The basic designs are called key types or plates.

Kiloware Stamps on paper that are sold by weight are called kiloware.

Maximum Card A postcard which features the design of the stamp or an enlarged picture of it.

Miniature Sheet One value or set printed in a special mini-sheet for collectors.

BELOW A miniature sheet showing one stamp as part of the design.

Mint Technically a mint stamp is in the same condition as when it was sold at the post office. However, the term is often applied to any unused stamps. Many dealers use the term 'mint' to describe unused stamps in a range of conditions

Multipositive One of the printing plates used in the photogravure printing method.

Off-set If the printing ink is still damp when the sheets are stacked, part or all of the design appears on the gum of the top sheet.

Overprint A surcharge or text printed on to a stamp.

Paquebot A letter posted at sea will use the stamps from the last port of call or the country of origin.

Perfin At one time some companies had their initials perforated into their stamps to prevent unauthorized use by employees. These are most easily seen from the back of the stamp.

Phosphor Band To activate automatic letter-facing machines a phosphorescent material was printed in bands on the stamps.

Plate Proof An imperforate trial sheet from a new plate to be checked for flaws.

Precancel Stamps which have a cancellation applied before being used for postage. Usually only applies to

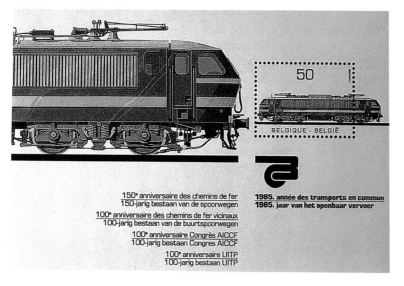

American stamps, which show the name of the post office between horizontal lines.

Pre-Stamp Cover A letter sent before the introduction of adhesive postage stamps.

Proof An impression of a stamp made by the printers during the preparation of the printing plates.

Provisionals Stamps produced locally to overcome a shortage of certain national values.

Rate Mark The cost of sending a letter written or hand-stamped on the front of the letter.

Remainders An occasional practice during the last century was for postal authorities to sell off surplus stocks to dealers at discounted prices. When stamps have been remaindered the catalogue value for unused examples is usually much less than that of used stamps.

Reprint Later printings of postage stamps were sometimes produced for collectors.

Se-tenant Stamps of different values printed side by side.

Space-Filler This term refers to a damaged stamp mounted in a collection until such a time when a better example can be found to replace it.

Specimen A stamp overprinted 'SPECIMEN' when it is sent out for promotional or similar purpose.

BELOW An overprint specimen on imperforate King George V 1d stamps.

Most specimen stamps occurred between the 1870s and 1940s when the Universal Postal Union needed examples of every new stamp to send to all the participating nations. Nowadays the only specimens are manufactured by a small number of countries as part of their press releases or for give-away promotions.

Surcharge A new value is overprinted on an existing stamp, usually because supplies of a particular value have run low or a new postage rate is introduced.

LEFT A Strip of se-tenant stamps.

Tête-bêche Two stamps printed together but with one design printed upside down. They come from sheets printed for booklets.

Tied A stamp is said to be tied to a cover when the postmark covers both the stamp and the cover. This proves that the stamp belongs to the cover.

Traffic Lights Sheets of stamps usually show cylinder numbers at one side with coloured circles on the other.

Transit Marks Postmarks applied to a cover between posting and delivery. It was usual for all mail to be postmarked each time it was sorted and international letters might receive two or three transit marks.

Underprint Text printed on the back of a stamp. In Britain underprints were used before the introduction of perfins. In these cases the name of the company was printed on the paper before it was gummed. Later British examples of underprints were printed on top of the gum. In 1893 stamps of New Zealand were issued with a variety of commercial advertisements on the back. They were printed before the stamps were gummed and can be collected in used condition. Advertisements for Pear's Soap, used as experiments in the 1890s are also available.

Unmounted Mint An unused stamp which has not been mounted with a stamp hinge, so that the gum is in perfect condition.

Used Abroad When a stamp from one country has been used in one of its postal agencies in a foreign country, it is said to have been used abroad.

Vignette Labels applied to covers which typically advertise an event associated with the cover, or give special instructions.

Watermark An impressed pattern made in the paper during its manufacture. The watermark can be seen as a slight thinning of the paper in a regular pattern.

Wrapper A sheet of paper folded around a letter and fastened with wax or a special seal. Wrappers were used before envelopes became cheap enough for general use.